The Usborne Book of
Poems for
Little Children

Designed by Amanda Gulliver
and Matt Durber

The Usborne Book of Poems for Little Children

Collected by Sam Taplin

Illustrated by Masumi Furukawa

In this book, I've collected some very special poems for you. Poems really come to life when you speak them and hear the music of their words, so try reading them out loud. Feel the beat of their rhythms and enjoy the sound of their rhymes. You might want to say them slowly and softly, or quickly and noisily – see what feels right to you. Have fun finding your own way of saying each one.

Sam Taplin

Contents

6   Pitter-patter Raindrops

8   Gorilla!

10   New Snow

12   Cow

14   When I was Three

15   Up to the Ceiling

16   Cats

18   What a Nose!

20   What will the Weather be like Today?

22   Oink! Baa! Cluck! Quack! Moo!

24   Under a Stone

25   Stepping Stones

26   Mice

28   Mud

30   Moving Away

32   On the Beach

34   Nobody Loves Me

36   Five Little Monkeys

38   Hiding

39   Something About Me

40   Into the Bathtub

42   The Bestest Bear Song

44   This Tooth

45   Two in Bed

46   Bedtime

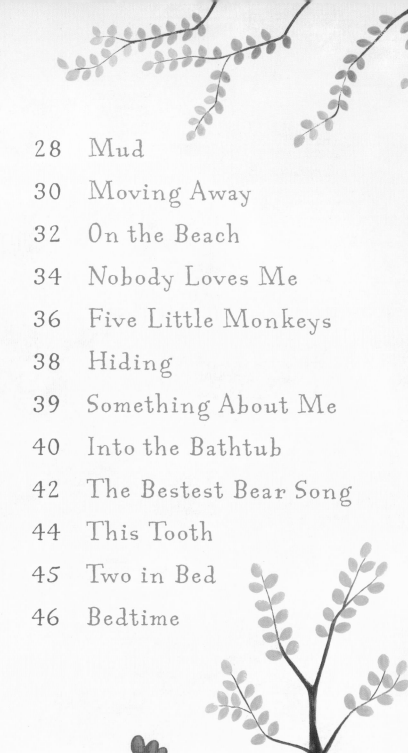

Pitter-patter Raindrops

I hear thunder.

I hear thunder.

Hark! Don't you?

Hark! Don't you?

Pitter-patter, raindrops,

Pitter-patter, raindrops.

I'm wet through,

So are you!

Gorilla!

I'm a Gorilla!

I'm a Gorilla!

I want ice cream

And I want vanilla!

Three big scoops

On a dish with a spoon.

I want ice cream

And I want it SOON.

Kaye Umansky

8

New Snow

The new new snow
is sparkling
in the sun.

Wherever I go
in the new new snow
I am
the
very
first one!

Lilian Moore

Cow

Sometimes I moo while I'm chewing

I hope you don't think that it's rude.

But mooing and chewing

Are what I like doing,

Do you moo when you chew your food?

Giles Andreae

When I was Three

When I was three I had a friend
Who asked me why bananas bend,
I told him why, but now I'm four
I'm not so sure...

Richard Edwards

Up to the Ceiling

Daddy lifts me
up to the ceiling.
Daddy swings me
down to the floor.
Daddy! Daddy!
More! More! MORE!
Up to the ceiling,
down to the floor.

Charles Thomson

Cats

Cats sleep
Anywhere,
Any table,
Any chair,
Top of piano,
Window-ledge,
In the middle,
On the edge,

Open drawer,
Empty shoe,
Anybody's
Lap will do,
Fitted in a
Cardboard box,
In the cupboard
With your frocks –
Anywhere!
They don't care!
Cats sleep
Anywhere.

Eleanor Farjeon

17

What a Nose!

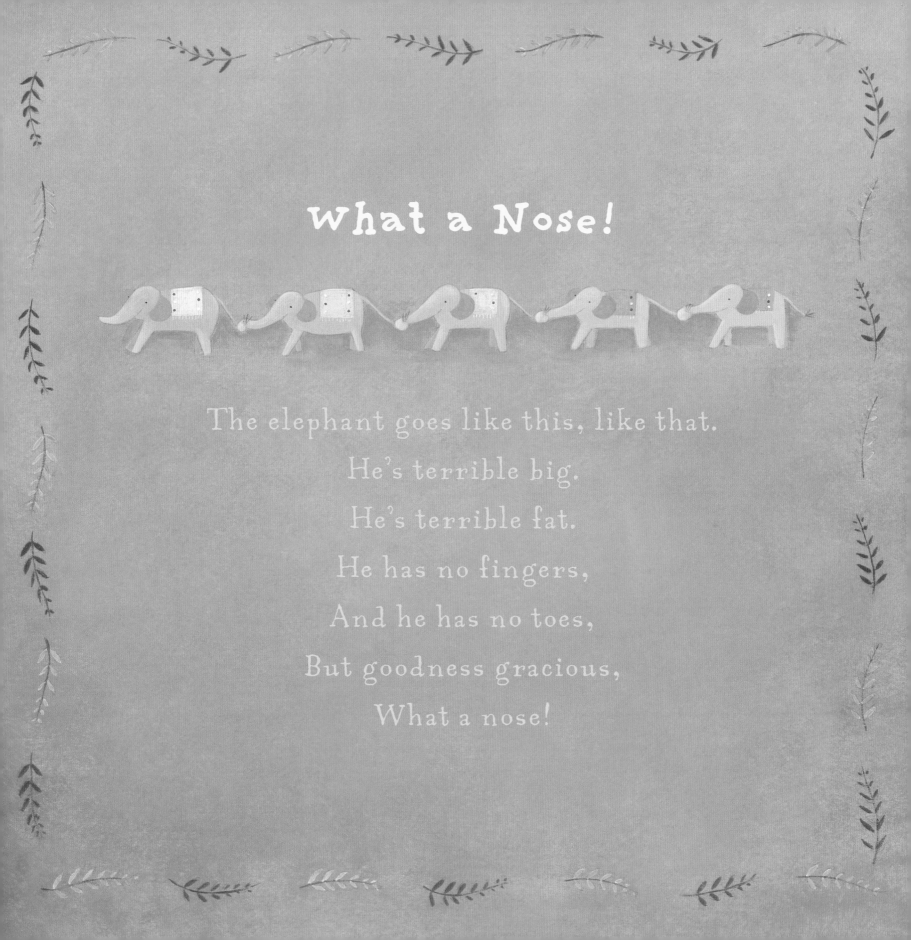

The elephant goes like this, like that.

He's terrible big.

He's terrible fat.

He has no fingers,

And he has no toes,

But goodness gracious,

What a nose!

what will the Weather be like Today?

Just at the moment
when night becomes day,
when the stars in the sky
begin fading away,
you can hear all the birds
and the animals say,
"What will the weather
be like today?"

Will it be windy?
Will it be warm?
Will there be snow?
Or a frost?
Or a storm?

"Be dry," says the lizard,
"and I won't complain."
The frog in the bog says,
"Perhaps it will rain."

The white cockatoo
likes it steamy and hot.
The mole doesn't know
if it's raining or not.
"Whatever the weather,
I work," says the bee.
"Wet," says the duck,
"is the weather for me."
"Weather? What's that?"
say the fish in the sea.

The world has awoken.
The day has begun,
and somewhere it's cloudy,
and somewhere there's sun,
and somewhere the sun
and the rain meet to play,
and paint a bright rainbow
to dress up the day!

How is the weather
where you are today?

Paul Rogers

Oink! Baa! Cluck! Quack! Moo!

I went to visit a farm one day
And saw a *pig* across the way.
Now what do you think I heard it say?

Oink! Oink! Oink!

I went to visit a farm one day
And saw a *sheep* across the way.
Now what do you think I heard it say?

Baa! Baa! Baa!

I went to visit a farm one day
And saw a *hen* across the way.
Now what do you think
I heard it say?

Cluck! Cluck! Cluck!

22

I went to visit a farm one day
And saw a *duck* across the way.
Now what do you think I heard it say?

Quack! Quack! Quack!

I went to visit a farm one day
And saw a *cow* across the way.
Now what do you think
I heard it say?

Moo! Moo! Moo!

I went to visit a farm one day
And saw *all* the animals
across the way.
Now what do you think
I heard them say?

Oink! Baa! Cluck!
Quack!
Moo-o-oo!

23

Under a Stone

Under a stone
Where the earth was firm,
I found a wiggly, wriggly worm;
"Good morning," I said.
"How are you today?"

But the wriggly worm just wriggled...
...away!

Stepping Stones

Stepping over stepping stones,
one, two, three,
Stepping over stepping stones,
come with me.
The river's very fast
And the river's very wide
And we'll step on stepping stones...

...and reach the other side.

Mice

I think mice
Are rather nice.
Their tails are long,
Their faces small,
They haven't any
Chins at all.
Their ears are pink,
Their teeth are white,

They run about
The house at night.
They nibble things
They shouldn't touch
And no one seems
To like them much.

But *I* think mice
Are nice.

Rose Fyleman

Mud

I like mud.

    I like it on my clothes.

I like it on my fingers.

    I like it in my toes.

Dirt's pretty ordinary

    And dust's a dud.

For a really good mess-up

    I like mud.

John Smith

Moving Away

My best friend's leaving school
today,
she's moving somewhere new.
Her house is on the market,
her brother's going too...

30

I saw the truck that was loading
her toys
her coat
her hat...
her bike
and books
and bedclothes
her hamster and her cat.

She said –
    she'd come and see me,
I said –
    I'd go and see her,
but I don't like these changes
    I liked things as they were.

Peter Dixon

31

On the Beach

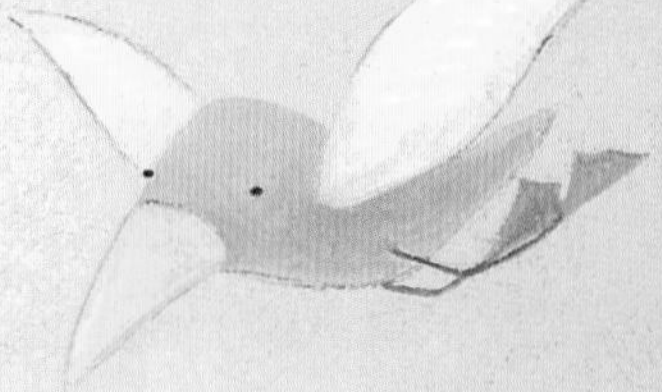

They buried their dad
in the golden sands,
buried his legs,
buried his hands,
buried his body
and buried his toes
and left just his face
and a very red nose.

Marian Swinger

Nobody Loves Me

Nobody loves me,
Everybody hates me,
I think I'll go and eat worms.

Big fat squishy ones,
Little thin skinny ones,
See how they wriggle and squirm.

Bite their heads off.
"Schlurp!" they're lovely,
Throw their tails away.

Nobody knows
How big I grows
On worms three times a day.

Five Little Monkeys

Five little monkeys
Walked by the shore,
One sailed off –
So that left four.

Four little monkeys
Climbed up a tree.
One fell down –
So that left three.

Three little monkeys
Found some sticky glue.
One got stuck in it –
So that left two.

Two little monkeys
Found a currant bun.
One ran off with it –
So that left one.

One little monkey
Worked hard all afternoon.
He built himself a spaceship –
And flew off
to the moon.

Hiding

Behind this tree
You can't see me,
I've made myself thin
So I can fit in.

I'm still as a photograph,
As quiet as a blink,
I won't sniff or laugh
Just quietly think.

Behind this tree
You can't see me,
I've made myself thin
So I can fit in.

Coral Rumble

Something About Me

There's something about me

That I'm knowing.

There's something about me

That isn't showing.

I'm growing!

Into the Bathtub

Into the bathtub,
Great big splosh.
Toes in the bathtub,
Toes in the wash.

Soap's very slidy,
Soap smells sweet.
Soap all over,
Soap on your feet.

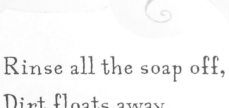

Rinse all the soap off,
Dirt floats away.
Dirt in the water.
Water's gone grey.

Out of the bathtub,
Glug, glug, glug.
Great big towel,
Great big hug.

Wendy Cope

The Bestest Bear Song

Oh,

this is the

bear,

the very best

bear,

the best *bestest* best

bear

of all.

It's lost one leg

and it's lost one eye

and it's spotty

and it's grotty

and it's small.

But
this is the
bear,
the very best
bear,
the best *bestest* best
bear
of all.
Yes, Sir!

Wes Magee

This Tooth

I jiggled it
jaggled it
jerked it.

I pushed
and pulled
and poked it.

But –

As soon as I stopped,
And left it alone,
This tooth came out
On its very own!

Lee Bennett Hopkins

44

Two in Bed

When my brother Tommy

Sleeps in bed with me,

He doubles up

and makes

himself

exactly

like

a

V

And 'cause the bed is not so wide,

A part of him is on my side.

Abram Bunn Ross

Bedtime

Five minutes, five minutes more, please!
Let me stay five minutes more!
Can't I just finish the castle
I'm building here on the floor?
Can't I just finish the story
I'm reading here in my book?
Can't I just finish this bead-chain –
It *almost is* finished, look!
Can't I just finish this game, please?
When a game's once begun
It's a pity never to find out
Whether you've lost or won.

Can't I just stay five minutes?
Well, can't I stay just four?
Three minutes, then? Two minutes?
Can't I stay one minute more?

Eleanor Farjeon

Index of First Lines

38 Behind this tree	30 My best friend's leaving school
16 Cats sleep	34 Nobody loves me
15 Daddy lifts me	42 Oh this is the bear
36 Five little monkeys	12 Sometimes I moo while I'm chewing
46 Five minutes, five minutes more	25 Stepping over stepping stones
6 I hear thunder	18 The elephant goes like this, like that
8 I'm a Gorilla!	10 The new new snow
44 I jiggled it	39 There's something about me
28 I like mud	32 They buried their dad
40 Into the bathtub	24 Under a stone
26 I think mice	14 When I was three I had a friend
22 I went to visit a farm one day	45 When my brother Tommy
20 Just at the moment	

Acknowledgements

Every effort has been made to trace the copyright holders of the material in this book, but this has not been possible in all cases. If any rights have been omitted, the publishers offer to rectify this in any subsequent editions following notification. The publishers are grateful to the following individuals and organizations for their permission to reproduce copyright material.

8 "Gorilla!" by Kaye Umansky from *Nonsense Animal Rhymes* (OUP, 2001). © Kaye Umansky 2001. Reprinted by permission of Oxford University Press.

10 "New Snow" by Lilian Moore. © 2001 Lilian Moore. From the book *I'm Small and Other Verses* by Lilian Moore, illustrated by Jill McElmurry. Reproduced by permission of Walker Books Ltd, London SE11 5HJ.

12 "Cow" by Giles Andreae. Reprinted by permission of PFD on behalf of: Giles Andreae.

14 "When I Was Three" by Richard Edwards. First published in *The Word Party* (Lutterworth Books, 1986). Reprinted by permission of the author.

15 "Up to the Ceiling" by Charles Thomson. Reprinted by permission of the author.

16 "Cats" by Eleanor Farjeon. Reprinted by permission of David Higham Associates.

20 "What will the Weather be like Today?" by Paul Rogers. Reprinted by permission of Hachette Children's Books.

26 "Mice" by Rose Fyleman. Reprinted by permission of the Society of Authors as the Literary Representative of the Estate of Rose Fyleman.

30 "Moving Away" by Peter Dixon. From *The Penguin in the Fridge* (Macmillan, 2000). Reprinted by permission of the author.

32 "On the Beach" by Marian Swinger, taken from *Read Me First* (Macmillan, 2003). Reprinted by permission of Macmillan Publishers Ltd.

38 "Hiding" by Coral Rumble. First published in *A Year of Rhymes* (Pan Macmillan, 2002). Reprinted by permission of the author.

40 "Into the Bathtub" by Wendy Cope. Reprinted by permission of PFD on behalf of: Wendy Cope. © Wendy Cope 1999.

42 "The Bestest Bear Song" by Wes Magee. Reprinted by permission of the author.

46 "Bedtime" by Eleanor Farjeon. Reprinted by permission of David Higham Associates.

Cover Design by Francesca Allen.